NO MORE CHAINS:
POETIC TESTIMONIES

By

Dawana Parks-Seabrook

authorHOUSE®

AuthorHouse™
1663 Liberty Drive
Bloomington, IN 47403
www.authorhouse.com
Phone: 1-800-839-8640

First published by AuthorHouse   10/19/2010

ISBN: 978-1-4520-6413-0 (e)
ISBN: 978-1-4520-6414-7 (sc)

Printed in the United States of America
Bloomington, Indiana

This book is printed on acid-free paper.

I give special thanks to Jesus Christ, my Lord and Savior. I would also like to thank my family and friends for their patience, understanding, love and support. I love you all.

Dawana Parks-Seabrook began writing poetry at the age of eight years old. Though this is her first published book, she has written hundreds of poems. Dawana hopes readers will enjoy reading her poetry; understand the messages; and apply them to daily life. It is her goal to bring others to Christ through her poetry and testimony.

Dawana is married and is the proud mother of three. When she is not working as a substitute teacher or spending time with family and friends, she is reading inspirational work or writing poetry. Her passions include writing and working with individuals who have special needs.

Dawana strives to be a better person each day and pray that she leaves a good impression wherever she goes or in whatever she does. She not only write to inspire, but write poetry for others and events for a cause.

If you have any comments or requests, you may reach her at daw.banks@comcast.net.

CONTENTS

No More Chains I

There were no windows, no doors to break free.

I was shackled, locked down, life's chains had me.

Past pain and abuse I once had to endure

left me fearful, lonely, wounded and insecure.

I was always worried, restless, and stressed.

Disappointments had me hopeless and depressed.

I tried to escape the feelings with all my might,

but I grew weary as I continued to fight.

I just couldn't seem to break away, that is, until one extraordinary day.

It was the day I heard God speak, with great authority, not at all weak.

He said: my dear child, you can't do it alone. I shivered as the voice sent chills through my bones.

Then God lowered his voice and he said to me, I am the only one, who can help you break free.

If you just call on my name and take my holy hand. I will set you free into a whole new land.

I can exonerate your troubles and take worries away, if you just believe in me, have faith, and pray.

Accept me, believe, and your sins….. do confess. For I have the power to give you rest.

Apply my word daily, as each day pass. That's another step closer to the new land's grass.

A beautiful life in eternity, where there are no more chains and you will finally be free.

Breathe New Life into Me

Breathe new life into me
That I may begin to see
a new light spiritually.

Show me what I am to be
Serving you wholehearted
and faithfully.

Help me to love unconditionally
And be forgiving so I will feel free
of bondage and adversity.

Oh Lord, I cry out to thee
for you to breathe new
life into me.

Spiritual Alterations

I am not what I ought to be,

but

I am working on getting there.

I am not what I used to be

thanks

to prayer after prayer.

I just have to take each day one day at a time

all while keeping God's word

in my heart and on my mind.

John 3:30 says, "He must increase, but I must decrease".

and in doing so, it shall bring about peace.

While God increases in me the world will see

a transformation

as my heart and mind accept his spiritual alterations.

Isaiah 54:18

There was a trap set for me

But I went another route.

I chose the Lord's way without a shadow of a doubt.

I bumped into an organized weapon

certainly meant to explode

God quickly shielded me

and set me on another road.

I ended up slipping and falling into

a weapon into being.

All the while my vision was blurred

Now, I had trouble seeing.

I stopped and begin calling on our

Christ Lord and Savior's name

Jesus!!! Please protect me

And once again he came.

At last, I see and understand

what the scripture means

from the book of

Isaiah chapter **54** and verse **18**

No weapon formed against me shall prosper

In any way

If I follow Jesus' footstep, have faith,

And continue to pray.

(**Inspired by a sermon given by Rev. Nathaniel Lee**)

Thank You: My Shining Star

I looked towards the sky with a deep stare

and

begin speaking to my Lord in a thankful prayer:

Thank you God for blessing me

with the opportunity to get to know thee.

I know that you are the Superior one.

Thank you God for sending your son.

Thank you God, for your grace and mercy

And

For the agape love that you always show me.

Thank you God for being who you are,

My Father, protector, provider,

My Shining Star.

My Angel

I have an angel that stands by my side.
My angel walks with me as I take each stride.

My angel watches me each day and night
and
is careful to keep me in the blessed light.

I have an angel who watches my every move
And helps me remember to show myself approved.

God sent this angel to protect me throughout my days
and
Deter me from those temptations and ungodly ways.

My angel is my guidance and my spiritual friend,
who will go on watching me until the very end.

The Devil's Goal

The devils' goal is to kill, steal, and destroy on each and everyday.
So please don't let him steal your joy, nor take your hope away.

He will slither through the smallest cracks to have his way with
you.
He will happily begin the evil attacks and laugh as you struggle
through.

So what you do when you discover you are under attack......
Is to call on Jesus boldly and he will have your back.

Say: Dear Lord help me to put Satan under my feet.
Watch Satan flee because he knows God can never be beat.

Yes, Satan will flee and try to hide away,
That is until tomorrow, yes, the very next day.

He may try you again or someone else in your house
It could be your child or even your spouse.

Don't fret just keep being a warrior in prayer
and have faith and acknowledge that God is really there.

Pray for the protection of your family and friends
and even for your enemies to turn away from sin.

Don't let the devil win by reaching his ultimate goal, which is to
destroy a life no matter what sex, race, or how old.

God's Word

Let the pureness of God's word
Enlighten your eyes.
Have faith in God,
for his love never dies.

Let the perfectness of God's words
Rejoice in your heart.
Don't allow the devil to tear
that relationship apart.

After all, God is number one
And he is the right way.
Remember the devil is a liar
And will try to make you sway.

Remember to ask in Jesus name
As you kneel down to pray,
Ask our father to protect us
and keep the devil away.

Let us store in our hearts God's words and we will see,
Just how awesome our Lord, God can be.

The Law, the Bible, the Word

The law of the Lord, the Bible, the Word....
For someone not to believe seems quite absurd.

Perfect is how the Bible describes God's word....
Have you read it, studied it, or even heard....
How the law of our God has converted many souls
And how his word has touched the young and the old.

Do you not know that God's word is for sure...
Its purpose is to guide us and make our minds and hearts pure.

God's word is true and it is the only right way....
We must keep it and practice following it each day.

After all, it is the guide God has left us to live by...
We must treasure it wholeheartedly until the day we die.

A Whisper from God

I heard a whisper in my ear. Oh, how sweet the sound.
It whispered: Child, have no fear, it is I, the Father, you have found.

I am here and ready to take you in my arms...
To hold, comfort, and protect you from any harm.

Then the voice said: Don't worry, have faith. The first one to seek is I.
My child take heed to my words which I've left you to live by.

These words cover things that you may face in life....
They will carry you through any tribulations and strife.

My word speaks on childhood to adulthood and other things we should know.
Study and believe in my word and on your mind and heart it should grow.

Again, I heard a whisper in my ear.
Oh how sweet the sound.
It whispered: child my kingdom is near
And it is I, your Father you have found.

A...C...T...S

A.......... IS FOR ADORATION...UNTO THE LORD WE MUST DISPLAY.

C..........IS FOR CONFESSION...ASK FOR FORGIVENESS IN A SINCERE WAY.

T..........IS FOR THANKS; WE MUST THANK GOD EVERYDAY.

S..........IS FOR SUPPLICATION, ON BEHALF OF OTHERS WE SHOULD PRAY.

Thank You Lord

Thank you Lord for these past years
as you guided me through the troubles and tears.

There were times it seemed you didn't care,
But deep inside I knew you were there.

Unlike man, you didn't leave me high and dry,
But you stayed and comforted me as the days went by.

Lord, I thank you for your amazing grace
And for your constant care and warm embrace.

I will continue to thank you to the very end,
because in you I have indeed found a friend.

Not only are you my friend, but you are my father, provider,
protector, and the head of my life.
Thank you for providing, protecting me, and bringing me through
trials, tribulations, and strife.

```
        E
       S
      I
    R
  A
```

ARISE!!!!...................above obstacles in your path
That seems to be cluttering your way.

ARISE!!!!...................above the curses planted and
negatives things people have to say.

ARISE!!!!...................above matters that are pressing
on your mind.

ARISE!!!!...................above losing yourself due to
things you've had to leave behind.

ARISE!!!!...................above things you've done or did
not do.

ARISE!!!!...................for your season has come and
the Glory of the Lord is risen upon you.

Inspired by ISAIAH 60:1

Take a Chance on Jesus

I thought there was nobody I could turn to, but there Jesus surfaced.
I saw nothing meaningful to do, but he gave me purpose.

The enemy rose fiercely against me and tried to weigh me down,
But, there he stood gracefully in his beautiful Holy crown.

I reached out to Jesus and boldly called his name.
He grabbed my hand securely and guided me as I came.

He assured me that everything would be okay,
as long as I believed and walked with him each day.

So when you think you are alone and you feel you're in despair,
just call on Jesus, for he will always be there.

Jesus will help you with whatever the situation.
Whether it be confusion, loneliness, or desolation,

If you haven't already, take a chance on Jesus, he is waiting on you.
It is the most important and rewarding thing you could ever do.

A LOVE.....

A love of manifestation that overcomes all situations.....covers all sins, never fails, never ends.....edifies minds and hearts, restores, giving new starts.....reaches beyond all things, what a wonderful aroma it brings.....turns frowns upside down.....smiles on faces, deliverance from dire places.....

A love of giving to help others, an act of blessing our sisters and brothers.....doing meaningful deeds by helping those in need......a kind word, which some have never heard..... a prayer to touch and heal those who are weak and ill.....
an invitation to Christ, to a lost soul or one's life.....
A love of all love decanted from our Heavenly Father above.

LOVE IS WHAT MAKES THE WORLD GO AROUND

Red may be the color of love......

......like a full bloomed rose......

.......or maybe love is as blue as the sky above......

.......the color of love..........nobody knows.

Love may feel like a cotton ball......

......very soft to one's touch......

.......or does love even have a feeling at all......

......Yes! Sometimes the feeling is too much.

Love may taste like caramel candies......

or perhaps like the frosting on a cake......

.......maybe love tastes like Pecan Sandies......

........or like the butter roll my mama makes.

Love may have many sounds like tunes from a radio.....

........the tunes may go up and other times down.......

.......There is one thing that I certainly know......

GOD'S LOVE IS WHAT MAKES THE WORLD GOES AROUND!!!!!!!!!

WORRY NOT……..

Worry not……the Lord knows your needs
He knows our sinful ways as well as our good deeds.

The Lord knows us, inside and out……yes, our entire lives, he
knows about.

He knows what we will do, even before it is done.
We can't fake it, fool him, hide, or run.

The Lord knows all, for he is the most high.
So trust and believe in him as each day passes by.

Worry not….. our Lord and Savior has your back.
Just stay focused and remain on the right track.

SWEET JESUS

My Jesus grows sweeter and sweeter each day passes by. He never ceases to amaze me and here are reasons why:

1. When I am confused, he enlightens me.

2. When I'm blinded by the world, he enables me to see.

3. When I am feeling trapped, he provides a way out.

4. Nobody understands me, but he knows what I am about.

5. When I am afraid, he takes away the fear.

6. When I am feeling lonely, he lets me know he is near.

7. When I am feeling sad, he reverses my frown.

8. When I am angry, he always calms me down.

9. There may be times when it seems I can't continue,

10. but my sweet Jesus always comes to my rescue.

Trust in Him

No matter whether there are imperfections, when one walks with the Lord, he's headed in the right direction.

If one's heart is just and he fights the flesh, our mighty Lord will do the rest.

He will strengthen us in the areas where we are weak. He will make it possible to land on our feet.

There will be negative people, don't pay attention to them.
Keep your eyes on the Lord, and trust in him.

Don't Forget

I found myself in a valley and did not know what to do.
I had not one person whom I could turn to.
I was alone and I felt pretty sad.
I thought how in the world things could get so bad.
I whined and I wept until I was weak and then a voice said:

There is one you may seek.
Did you forget the one that gave you life and kept you
all these years?
Do you know that he can wipe away your tears?
Do you not know that he will restore what you have lost,
no matter how much or what it costs?
Do you not know he can heal all sickness and pain?
He can rationalize your mind when you are feeling insane.
Don't forget to thank and praise God in all you do.
He is one we can always turn to.

A State of Being

In a state God didn't intend for us to be.
Our eyes are wide open,
Yet we are unable to see.

We are blind to life and what we were put here to do.
Rather we focus on ourselves and things we are going
through.

We focus on the bad rather than the good.
We do things we shouldn't rather than things we should.

We whine about things we don't have, rather than thanking
God for the present blessings.
Instead of casting our cares upon him, we are busy stressing.

We go about our day, never stopping to pray,
never acknowledging our Lord and Savior.
No! God didn't intend for us to have such behavior.

So when will we open our eyes to see, the state in which God
intended for us to be.

I Am Sold!

I have climbed many hills and mountains to get where I am today. I thank God for each and every step of the way.

There was sweat and tears, but somehow I made it through. I am here to tell you to keep climbing and you will make it too.

No matter what the situation or what it looks like to the human eye. Just know that there are angels protecting you as you pass on by.

At the same time, there will be debris that will probably make you fall. Just get back up; continue your journey, giving it your all.

The hills and mountains may get steeper than they have been in the past. Then suddenly you have reached that point...to your destination at last.
I am here Lord, standing with all I have and hold. Thank you for your patience. Now to you I am sold.

Walk Diligently

Be diligent in your walk with Christ, our Lord and
Savior.
Be humble, faithful, and have a sincere virtuous
behavior.

Be Godly, kind, and loving in your talk
as you let go of old ways and experience a new walk.

Be knowledgeable, have self-control. In this walk, do
persevere.
And
As you go through the storms, to God's words adhere.

As for all negative words and acts, you should release
As you experience God's mercy, his grace and peace.

Inspired by 2 Peter 1

A Tribute to Mama

Mama, you had us all young and you had a lot to learn, but you knew how to love us children yet knew when to be stern.

You would laugh and play with us and teach us many things. Oh, I remember the good times when you would play records for us and sing.

I remember when you taught me to braid hair and how to ride a bike. I remember you taking me shopping to pick out things I liked.

You would cook the best meals and made homemade desserts. You did this even on the days you attended school or work.

Our lives were not perfect, for we had days that were bad, but I choose to focus on the good days we had.

I thank God for the time spent with my sister and brothers and I especially thank him for the blessing of having you as our mother.

Dedicated to my loving mother

Sisters Are a Blessing

Sisters are a joy to have, though they don't always
get along.
They sometimes squabble and disagree on who is
right or wrong.
The squabbles don't last due to love that conquers
all.
So, it is not a surprise when one sister makes that
"apologetic" call.
It's good to hear my sister's voice on the other end
of the phone.
That's where we bury the hatchet and let our by
gones be gone.
Yes, sisters can be difficult, but it is a blessing in
the end.
In a sister one can find a truly, great friend.
Wait! There is one more thing I need to say
before I am done.
One thing greater than having a sister, is to be
blessed with more than one.

L-O-V-E

L is for life...live it lively and lovingly while we are blessed with the

O pportunity to observe God's Omnipotence as we obey his word

and

V alue his vast grace and mercy Vivaciously

E ach and everyday exquisitely.

The Day I Meet Jesus

I dream of the day when I meet Jesus; as he sets me on his knee; he smiles and looks at me

and says: Well done, my child!

I dream of the day when Jesus takes my hand and looks into my eyes and I receive the prize

Of hearing him say: Well done, my child!

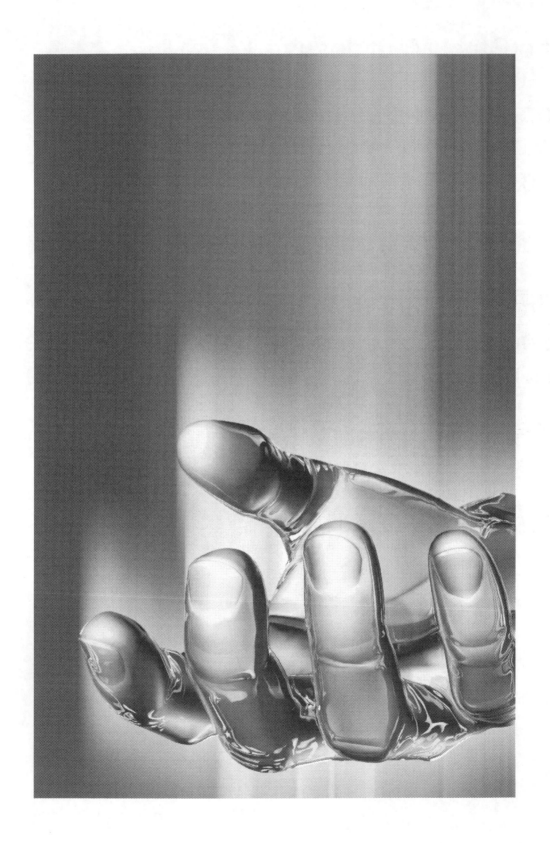

God's Open Hands

When your life is in shambles, and things are upside down,
God's love still stands.

It may not seem that God is around, but he's there standing with
open hands.

Don't have too much pride or be afraid to call his name.
In him you can confide, no need to be shy or shame.

You may have walked away from him, but God's love still stands.
He will always be there, waiting with open hands.

You can always trust that God will be there,
and it never hurts to send up a confession prayer.

Forgive me oh Lord for I have sinned in my heart.
I have fallen short of doing my part.

I pray that you strengthen me in my weak areas
and help me knock down those difficult barriers.

Lord, help me stay grounded and walk in your plan
and thanks for your loving, open hands.

LOVING and FORGIVING

There were feelings not expressed and words unsaid.
Faults were not confessed, stubbornness and animosity instead.

You never took the time to make up and forgive. Now it's the end of the line and the person no longer lives.

You never said "I love you" before he or she died. Now you don't know what to do and you're feeling terrible inside.

Repent with sincerity and keep on living,
And remember it's always good to be loving and forgiving.

You never know when your life will end or your loved one may be put to rest.

In the end, living, learning, and FORGIVING will always be the best.

Inspired by Colossians 3:13 and dedicated to those who find it hard to forgive.

MY STRENGTH, MY POWER and SOURCE

Direct me Oh Lord; let me hear your voice

For you are my strength; you are my source.

Open my ears that I may hear when you speak

Humble my spirit, so that I know when to be meek.

Open my eyes, so that I may see

the path that you have intended for me.

Train my voice to speak, knowing when and what to say.

Let my heart be filled with love each and everyday.

Lace my tongue with positive words to encourage

as I lift up those, who have been repeatedly discouraged.

Lord, guide me into obedience unto you,

so that I may know when and what to do.

Direct me Oh Lord, into making the right choice,

For you are my strength, you are my power and my source.

Chaotic Storms

Despite the chaotic storms, your life has not crumbled.

Tranquility has been formed is why you haven't stumbled.

At first, your heart was full of sorrow,

but now the burdens are released.

Rather than fretting about tomorrow,

You are living now…at peace.

You have given Jesus your heart and he is guiding the way.

You now have a new start and know in Christ you must stay.

Though the storms may be gone temporarily, they may come swarming through again.

Holding on to Jesus Christ vigorously will help you to the end.

Don't be afraid when the storms come, Jesus is on your side, waiting and smiling with his arms open wide.

Release the Negative

Tomorrow starts right now, so let change start today.

Examine yourself wholeheartedly in the most humble way.

Don't put things off tomorrow for today is just as good.

Procrastination is not the way, so start now, if you would.

From within, yes, please examine your heart and mind.

There will be good, though some negative you will find.

Don't let it be a discourage, but now that you are aware,

know that things can be fixed through fasting and the power of prayer.

Pray that Christ increases in you as the negative ways decrease.

Positive will soon take over as the negative is released.

Our Glorious King

Our Glorious King will help us through
when we are confused and don't know what to do.

He will help us feel better when we are feeling pretty low
and guide us when we don't know which way to go.

One might not believe and say "how could this be?" Well, listened to this
short story about me:

I was depressed and confused and on medication.
It all stemmed from childhood devastation.

The medicine made me feel numb or tired most days.
I thought how much longer could I go on this way?

Though my first marriage had failed, I had been blessed with a son.
For him I had to get better, I could not give up or run.

Though, I had done shameful things that I knew were not right,
I was determined the devil would not win this fight.

I couldn't do it alone and had to call on my King,
Not realizing what a great change it would bring.

As I sat alone, I heard a voice just as plain....
I thought maybe the medicine had me going insane?

I couldn't see anyone, but I felt someone was there,
so I fell on my face in a desperate prayer.

I praised God and asked forgiveness of my sins
of all the things I had done and places I had been.

I asked God to help me out of this dark valley of grief
And give me rest, restoration, and relief.

You see, God is able to change and provide all things.
For he is the most high, he is our Glorious King.

God Wants to Talk to Us

God wants to talk to us. But we won't sit long enough.

We are too busy to listen because we are doing other stuff.

God wants to talk to us but some of us have closed our ears,

while our lips are busy flapping and gossiping about our peers.

God wants to talk to us but some of us don't believe

that someone may be blocking us from that word we are to receive.

God wants to talk to us, but we haven't taken time to call his name.

Instead we are complaining about problems and who is to blame.

God wants to talk to us, but we still haven't stopped to hear.

However, he is still waiting for us, the bible makes it clear.

God wants to talk to us and wants us to listen to what he has to say.

But, we keep pushing him aside day after day.

It is time we make the decision to listen to his voice.

Time is winding down, so go on and make the right choice.

Obedience

Receive, treasure, and keep God's commands

Listen wholeheartedly, meditate and understand

The value of his words, knowledge and wisdom too

That will at some point in your lifetime be a blessing to you.

Share how it has helped you and will help others out there

Let them know how it got you through things you thought you couldn't bear.

Don't hide the many blessings you have to talk about.

Share how it has changed you inside and out.

Each of us really has a purpose in life

And that is to bring at least one, if not many souls to Christ.

Inspired by Proverbs 2:1-2

REMEMBER WHEN....

Remember when...back in the day when we were young girls and boys.

We had the most fun without the extravagant toys.

We would run, jump, and play throughout the neighborhood.

We would climb every tree that we thought we could.

Remember when...back in the day we would play the simple games.

Now we have technology and things just aren't the same.

"Hide and seek", "Mother May I", marbles, and jack stones.

What happened to dodge ball and kickball, those good old days are gone.

We didn't have a pool; we would use the hose to "get wet".

Or race in the fields "On your mark, get set".

We would play a game of "Red Light Green Light" just before night

but managed to make it in the house and beat the street light

Remember when...back in the day when we had respect for others.

Children would obey their parents and there was love among sisters and brothers.

Remember when...back in the day when we would borrow from the neighbors.

It wasn't a big deal because people didn't mind lending favors.

Remember when...back in the day when we sat as a family to eat.

Fathers were the head of the household, and mothers had the Queen's seat.

Children were respectful and well behaved most days.

They were grateful and obedient as they practiced Christian ways.

Remember when...back in the day when more people had good behavior.

Most of them knew and viewed Christ as their Lord and Savior.

Remember when...we acknowledged and thanked him as we would pray.

Well if you don't remember Christ, acknowledge and accept him today.

Peace

God has blessed me with a peaceful new start. Now it is time to make a change.

He has touched my mind and heart to the point my priorities are rearranged.

I see things in a different light than I did once before.

With the new and improved sight, I understand a lot more.

I think in a more mature and spiritual way than I did as a child.

I know now that I shouldn't be anxious, but to be patient and wait a while.

As the Holy Spirit leads me into the journey of this new life,

Happy and at peace I may be, even in the middle of strife.

Peace from Christ is giving me rest as I continue to face each test.

A peaceful mind.....a peaceful heart is a great part of my blessed new start.

No More Chains II

No more chains, I am not shackled anymore.

I'm feeling free as a bird and I am ready to soar.

It is great to be free from life's heavy chains.

The burdens were beginning to drive me insane.

I am spiritually filled and I am in a new place,

No longer feel the need to hide my face.

Despite the many tribulations, I am still here.

I am no longer feeling desperate or living in fear.

The sadness has ceased and there isn't anymore depression.

Once ashamed to admit sin, now practicing full confessions,

The chain of insecurities have been liquefied,

I am sporting a bolder and more confident side.

Now it is time for me to encourage my sisters and brothers,

By telling my story or testifying to others.

Yes!! No more chains, I am not shackled anymore.

I'm feeling free as a bird and I am ready to soar.

Acknowledgements

Sometimes we go through things in life that contributes to experiences of depression, anger, fear, and many other negative feelings. We may even do things we wouldn't normally do. It is important to remember that we do not have to live this way. We cannot let negative past experiences dictate our future negatively. I encourage others to grab hold of Jesus and never let go. No matter what the situation, God can fix it. Regardless of what others are doing or what has been done to us, it is our duty to do the right things in life. That is seeking God, following his word, and sharing the good news with others.

Despite the pain, suffering, and abuse I have experienced in life, I am thankful, I am not bitter, and has moved on in life. God has brought me through it all. He has given me the strength and courage to carry on and trust in him. Reverend Nathaniel Lee, would quote his favorite scripture from the bible, John 3:30. He must increase, but I must decrease". I want God's spirit to work more in me rather me allowing the flesh to take over. Though, I am not perfect, I practice getting better each day. As I continue seeking God, studying his word, and practicing living accordingly, God's spirit continues to grow in me. Reverend Grady Caldwell reminds us often of something in the Bible. "What's the best thing in the world" he would ask throughout his sermons. The congregation would say "understanding". You see, I do not have to understand why I had to go through some things in life. I just need to understand that I was brought through for a reason…that is to bring others to Christ. Whether it is through my testimony, poetry, conversation, or a kind act, it is my duty to share what God has done for me.

Once again, I give thanks and praise to Jesus Christ. Along the way, God has placed some very special people in my life. I would like to acknowledge and thank my loving husband, Antonio Seabrook; my children Deon Banks, Shon and Tionna Seabrook; My supportive parents Eugene and Annette Carley; my wonderful siblings: Leroy Parks, Ulysses Gilbert, Tamara Garner, and Freddie Hughley. I give thanks to the entire Hughley family. I would also like to thank Rev. Nathaniel Lee, First Lady Lee and the Zion family; Rev. Grady Caldwell, First Lady Caldwell and the New Mercy family; Rev. Randy Valimont, First Lady Valimont and Griffin First Assembly of God family. I give special thanks to my friends Lanea Johnson, Joyce Williams, Sherita Jones, Stephanie Goodwin, Margie Washington and Gloria Mccall. The Seabrook Family and William Whitner. For those not mentioned, I thank you for any kind acts or positive words you have contributed to my life. Thank you and God bless you all.